Cumbria Libraries

3 8003 04494 8164

KU-546-432

Dirty Rotten

Pirates

A TRULY REVOLTING GUIDE TO PIRATES & THEIR WORLD

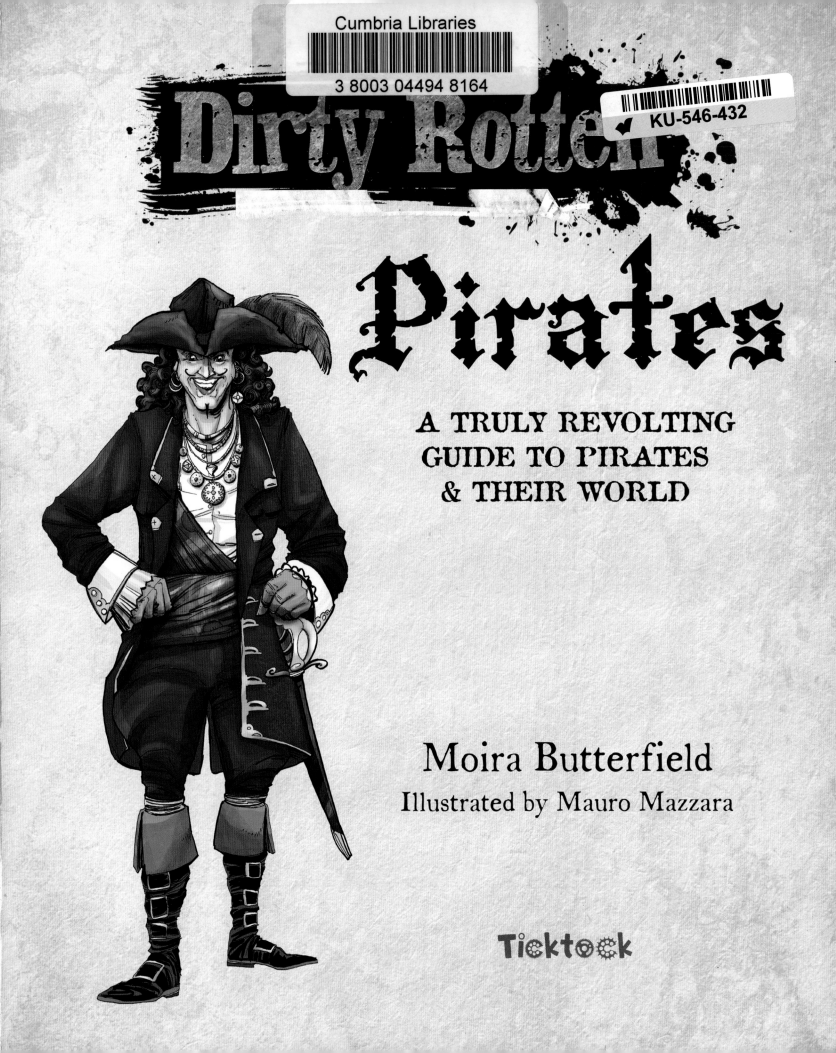

Moira Butterfield

Illustrated by Mauro Mazzara

Ticktock

An Hachette UK Company

www.hachette.co.uk

First published in Great Britain in 2014 by Ticktock,
an imprint of Octopus Publishing Group Ltd

Endeavour House
189 Shaftesbury Avenue
London
WC2H 8JY

www.octopusbooks.co.uk

www.ticktockbooks.co.uk

Copyright © Octopus Publishing Group Ltd 2014

All rights reserved. No part of this work may be reproduced or utilised in any form
or by any means, electronic or mechanical, including photocopying, recording
or by any information storage and retrieval system, without the prior written
permission of the publisher.

ISBN 978 1 78325 037 0

A CIP record for this book is available from the British Library

Printed and bound in China

1 3 5 7 9 10 8 6 4 2

Project Editor: Amanda Archer   Design: Perfect Bound Ltd
History consultant: Mark G Hanna, University of California, San Diego

Publisher: Samantha Sweeney Managing Editor: Karen Rigden
Senior Production Manager: Peter Hunt

LIBRARY SERVICES FOR SCHOOLS	
38003044948164	
Bertrams	27/06/2014
910.45	£6.99
LSS	

Contents

What is a Pirate Anyway?

There have been crooks roaming the seas ever since sailing began, thousands of years ago. We're going to enter the murky, mucky and decidedly stinky world of pirates!

GOVERNMENT PIRATES

In the 1500s pirates were semi-officially allowed. European countries paid privateers, sailors with privately-owned ships, to attack their enemies. They behaved like pirates, but they had an official licence to do it!

ANCIENT PIRATES

There were plenty of pirates in Roman times. They might have had to row their own ships, but it didn't stop them stealing plenty of stuff. They particularly liked kidnapping people and holding them for ransom.

Official Pirate Licence

'PROPER' PIRATES

Pirates with eye patches and cutlasses lived in the 1600s and 1700s, cruising the Caribbean and the coast of North America.

HEROES OR HORRORS?

Pirates of the past may sometimes seem brave and exciting, but real-life pirates led a tough and brutal life and weren't very nice people. If they didn't die from disease, they usually met a sticky end some other way!

Pirates Way Back When

If you think of a pirate, you'll imagine someone brandishing a cutlass, while saying 'Aharrr, me hearties. Mind me wooden leg!' This type of swashbuckler belongs to the Golden Age from 1690 to 1730, but there have been countless more types down the centuries, all partial to plundering.

ROMAN REVENGE

Around 75 BCE, Julius Caesar was captured and held hostage by Mediterranean pirates. He made friends with them, but as soon as he was released, hired ships and hunted them down. Pirates were crucified in Roman times, but legend has it that Caesar was merciful... sort of. He ordered their throats to be slit before they were nailed up.

HERE COME THE VIKINGS!

From the 800s to 1,000 AD, Viking marauders from Sweden, Norway, and Denmark plundered European coasts, stealing treasure and snatching people to sell as slaves.

They measured their wealth by the amount of precious metal they owned. The Vikings raided in longships called drakar, which means 'dragon'.

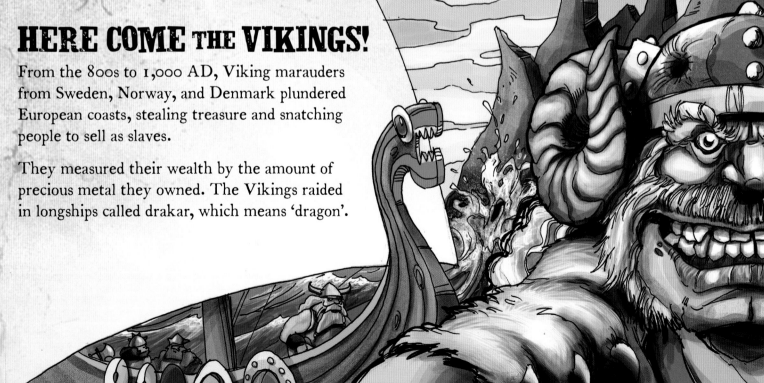

PIRATE PRIEST

Eustace the Monk was a medieval pirate known as the 'Black Monk'. With the agreement of England's King John, he raided French ships up and down the Channel. Later the ex-holy man swapped sides, and was paid by the French to fight the English.

Eustace met a painful end in 1217 when the English bombarded his ship with powdered lime. The lime formed a cloud of fog, blinding the crew.

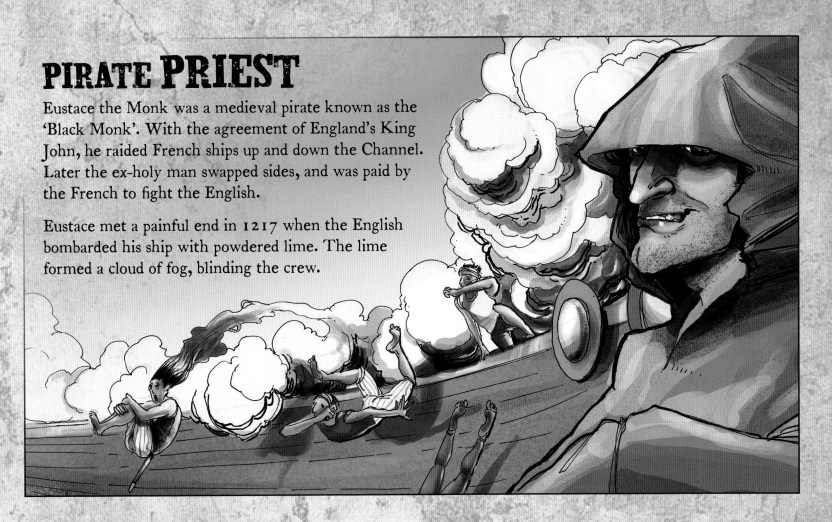

BALTIC BEER DRINKER

In the late 1300s, Klaus Störtebeker led a pirate band around the Baltic Sea. His surname meant 'emptying a jug of beer in one gulp'.

When captured, Störtebeker is said to have asked the Mayor of Hamburg to spare any crew members he could walk past after he had his head chopped off. Somehow he managed to stagger past twelve prisoners before the executioner tripped him up.

Sea Dogs or Scoundrels?

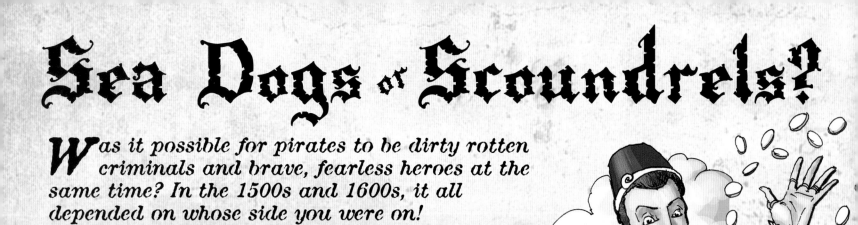

Was it possible for pirates to be dirty rotten criminals and brave, fearless heroes at the same time? In the 1500s and 1600s, it all depended on whose side you were on!

SPAIN FINDS TREASURE

In the 1500s, Spain took over Central and South America and began shipping back huge quantities of gold and silver on-board heavy cargo ships called galleons. Spain's European enemies decided to spoil the party by booking the services of their very own private pirates.

PERMISSION TO PLUNDER

The rulers of anti-Spanish nations such as England and the Netherlands issued licences, called Letters of Marque, giving permission for privately-owned ships to rob Spanish ports and ships in return for a cut of the booty. The freelance fighters were called 'privateers'.

PRIVATEER PARADE

Canny Queen Elizabeth I of England gave out lots of licences to British privateers, who were nicknamed 'Sea Dogs'. They raided Spanish ships and towns on her behalf and helped her to defeat the Spanish when they tried to invade England in 1588. Here are a few of her pirate-heroes:

RICHARD GRENVILLE was famed for his temper, as well as his fighting skills. He died when his men surrendered against his wishes after a twelve-hour sea battle with the Spanish in 1591.

WALTER RALEIGH was a hero who really lost his head. He was knighted by Queen Elizabeth but later beheaded by her successor, James 1, in 1618. The new king wanted to be friends with the Spanish, so Raleigh went from hero to zero.

FRANCIS DRAKE was a mega-hero to the English but a mega-monster to the Spanish. Their nickname for him was El Dragón – the dragon!

NO STOPPING THEM NOW!

The situation changed in the 1600s and Europe's rulers no longer needed their privateers, but many sailors decided to carry on mugging ships for money without permission from anyone.

Buccaneers Ahoy!

Aharrr, me hearties! Here comes the Golden Age, the name for the years between 1690 and 1730 when the kind of pirates we know from Hollywood movies roamed the oceans. Think peg legs, cutlasses and eye patches!

BARBECUE BOYS

From the late 1500s the island of Hispaniola (present day Haiti and the Dominican Republic) became home to a ragged band of runaway slaves and former French sailors. They lived as hunters, shooting wild pigs and smoking the meat on wooden frames called boucans. They got the name boucaniers, which later became 'buccaneers'.

The boucaniers used cutlasses to cut up the meat they hunted. It became the pirates' favourite weapon.

OUT OF CONTROL

The buccaneers were driven off Hispaniola by the Spanish and went to nearby Tortuga, where they were joined by fortune-seekers of all kinds. They were encouraged by Spain's enemies to raid Spain's treasure fleets and settlements, but soon they began attacking anyone who sailed by.

BEASTLY BUCCANEERS

Buccaneers were known for being cruel, especially Frenchman Francois L'Ollonais. This awful outlaw was known for torturing Spanish prisoners. It was even rumoured that he once cut out a victim's heart and forced somebody to eat it.

Some of the largest buccaneer raids were led by a Welsh captain called Henry Morgan. He got a privateer's license from the British and became a very wealthy man by raiding Spanish towns in the 1660s and 1670s. Morgan was knighted and even became the Lieutenant Governor of Jamaica, so piracy paid off for him!

A pirate surgeon called Alexandre Esquemeling wrote a book about the buccaneers he knew of, called *Bucaniers Of America*. His book was a bestseller in the 1600s.

Ye best seller of 1678!

BUCANIERS OF AMERICA

The Pirate Realm

This map shows the areas infected with pesky pirates from the age of the privateers through to the 1700s.

NORTH AMERICA

Gulf of Mexico

Havana

Veracruz

CENTRAL AMERICA

The Spanish conquered the Aztec and Inca civilizations living in Central and South America, and took all the fabulous gold and silver treasure they found. They melted down much of the metal to make silver coins called 'pieces of eight', and gold coins called 'doubloons'.

The Caribbean and the coast of North America provided lots of useful coves and bays where pirates could hide, waiting to pounce on unwary ships passing by.

Ocracoke

In the early days, the pirates' preferred victims were Spanish treasure galleons sailing from the Spanish Main, the coast of northern South America controlled by the Spanish.

N

The Spanish galleons sailed in large fleets to protect themselves from attack. Privateers cruised around looking for ships that had been separated from the fleet.

BAHAMAS

CUBA

Tortuga

JAMAICA Port Royal HISPANIOLA PUERTO RICO

(Now Haiti and The Dominican Republic)

The Caribbean Sea

Barbados

Cartagena

Trinidad

SOUTH AMERICA

Why Join the Pirates?

Why did men choose to be pirates? What made them join violent seagoing criminal gangs that sailed far from home and near to death?

NO-GOOD NAVY

British sailors sometimes chose piracy because Navy life was so awful. Many were forced to work on crowded ships, often getting cheated out of their wages. Navy captains were tough on their crew. No wonder pirates regularly renamed their captured ships *Revenge*!

DASTARDLY DICTIONARY of NAVY NASTINESS

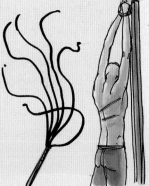

FLOGGING

Every man dreaded being flogged with a cat 'o' nine tails – a whip with nine knotted tails. It could scar someone for life.

KEEL-HAULING

This punishment saw a man being tied to a rope and pulled under the ship's hull, from one side to the other.

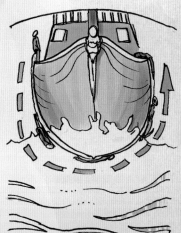

PRESS-GANGING

In England, men could be lawfully kidnapped by a Navy press gang. Many were seized from taverns and forced to sign up.

MUTINY

If your Navy captain was dreadful, you could mutiny – either killing him or setting him adrift in a boat.

JOIN US!

OR ELSE
When pirates captured a ship, they often forced sailors to join them, especially ones with valuable skills such as carpentry.

GET RICH... OR MAYBE NOT
Being a pirate might sound like an easy way to get wealthy, but in reality few ended up rich. Captured booty was more likely to be food, medical supplies or goods that had to be sold to make any money.

MAKE A LIVING
When peace came to Europe in the 1700s many sailors were thrown out of work, and life was very harsh if you were poor. Many ex-privateers had to turn pirate just to make ends meet.

BE FREE
Being a pirate meant freedom from tough government laws back home. If slaves were found on captured vessels they might be given the chance of freedom and allowed to become pirates themselves.

I'm in Charge!

After 1713 piracy went from bad to worse, with some crews even attacking their own nations! Most pirates voted for their own captain.

CHOOSING TIME

Thinking of applying for the job? Here's what you'll need to know! Many crews called a council to make important decisions. They would choose a captain for their leadership skills and expertise in finding ships to steal from.

CAPTAIN'S RULES

This is what a pirate crew would expect from a captain:

- Can you lead men into battle? You will make the decisions about chasing and attacking vessels.

- We'll decide everything else between us, thanks very much.

- You can't have any more food than the rest of us.

- Don't go thinking you're grander than us. You're not allowed to stay in your cabin all day long, thinking you're special.

- You must be prepared to attack and capture ships belonging to your former country.

IT'S ME, OR ELSE

Some captains didn't bother too much about fairness. They took control of their ships with threats of violence.

CAPTAIN BLACKBEARD is said to have shot members of his crew from time to time, just to show them who was in charge. Once, while playing cards with a crewman, he supposedly shot him under the table.

CAPTAIN EDWARD LOW was tough with his crew, too, and is said to have shot dead his second-in-command while he was sleeping. He once even made someone eat their own ears with salt and pepper! Eventually the crew dumped him overboard in a boat with no food. He was caught by French forces.

CAPTAIN CHEATER?

Rumour has it that Blackbeard deliberately ran his ship, *Queen Anne's Revenge*, aground so as to scatter his crew and take the loot on-board for himself. However, archaeologists have since discovered what they think is the shipwreck. It looks as if Blackbeard tried to save the ship and failed, so perhaps he wasn't quite as cunning as legends suggest.

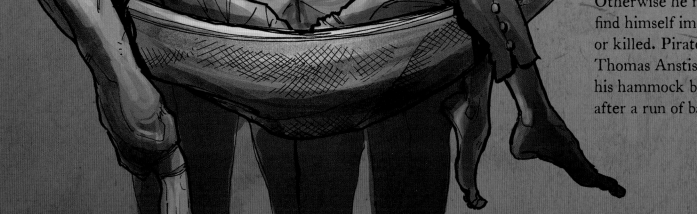

YOU'RE FIRED (REALLY)!

If a captain proved useless, he might be voted out and sent back to being an ordinary crew member. Otherwise he might find himself imprisoned or killed. Pirate leader Thomas Anstis was shot in his hammock by his crew after a run of bad luck.

Craziest Captains Ever

Many famous pirates were said to be a few coins short of a treasure pile. Were these crazy captains for real or was it all just an act to scare off their enemies? Here are some of the sailing celebrities of the Golden Age.

SMOKIN' TEACH!

Blackbeard was only a pirate captain for two years, around the Caribbean and North American Atlantic coast, but he went down fighting in a cloud of black smoke.

The pirate charged into battle with burning fuses in his hair, frightening victims into giving up their goods.

BLACKBEARD'S PECULIAR PIRATE FILE

- Blackbeard's real name was Edward Teach.
- He once cut off a prisoner's finger to snatch their diamond ring.

BONNET'S PECULIAR PIRATE FILE

- Bonnet was so useless that Blackbeard once tricked him out of his ship, crew and loot.
- He didn't even have a big bushy pirate beard. He wore a powdered wig and shaved!

THE POSHEST PIRATE

Stede Bonnet was once a wealthy gentleman in Barbados, but he suddenly bought a ship and became a pirate. At first he was a terrible sailor, and his crew left him to work for Blackbeard. Later he got better, but not good enough to avoid being hanged in 1718.

NO-HEART BART

'Black' Bart Roberts got his nickname from having black hair and dark skin. In a few short years between 1719 and 1722 he captured over 400 ships and got very rich, but he also earned a reputation for being mean and merciless.

ROBERTS' PECULIAR PIRATE FILE

- Roberts was forced to become a pirate when he was captured at sea.
- He preferred tea to alcohol.
- He was finally killed by a pirate-hunter's cannonball.

VANE'S PECULIAR PIRATE FILE

- Vane was shipwrecked on an island. Another pirate sailed past, but refused to rescue him because of his reputation.
- He was rescued by a captain who didn't know him, but later was recognized and arrested.

CASTAWAY CAPTAIN

Charles Vane joined a pirate crew in 1716 and was soon plundering ships. Vane was once voted out of the captaincy of his ship by his crew, who cast him away in a small boat.

WHO SAID THAT?

If some pirate captain stories seem far-fetched, it's probably down to the authors who wrote up their lives at the time. They may have exaggerated the truth, knowing that scandal sold books. We'll never know, me hearties!

The Pirate Code

They might have been a scurvy bunch of outlaws, but many Golden Age pirates stuck to a surprising number of rules.

DO AS YOU'RE TOLD

Crew members were expected to sign Articles of Agreement – a strict pirate code that listed the dos and don'ts on-board. Anyone who broke the Articles could expect punishment.

SIGN AND SWEAR

Some men swore their allegiance on a Bible, others on an axe. Only a few crew members with very important jobs, such as carpenters and surgeons, weren't forced to sign the Articles. Men who had not signed had a better chance of being let off if they were caught and tried as pirates.

SIGN HERE

Here is a modern, shortened version of the Articles that 'Black' Bart Roberts made his crew sign.

The ARTICLES

Article 1: Every man shall have an equal vote on-board. Everyone will get an equal share of food and strong drink, and won't have to share it unless supplies run low.

Article 2: Every man shall get a fair share of stolen treasure, but if anyone cheats by so much as one coin they will be marooned.

Article 3: Nobody will gamble for money on-board ship.

Article 4: All lights and candles must be put out by 8pm. Anyone who wants to stay up drinking after that must go on-deck in the dark.

Article 5: Every man must keep his weapons clean and ready for action.

Article 6: Anyone who tries to smuggle a woman on-board will be killed.

Article 7: Anyone who deserts during a battle will be killed or marooned.

Article 8: No crew members are allowed to fight each other on-board. They must settle their fight on the shore with pistols or cutlasses.

Article 9: Anyone who gets injured will be paid compensation. The worse the injury, the higher the payment.

Article 10: The most important members of the crew will get the biggest share of the plunder.

Article 11: The musicians on-board are allowed to rest on Sunday.

Who's Who in the Crew?

Pirates took their jobs seriously. If a pirate ship was badly organised, everybody's life was in danger. Here's your chance to meet the most important members of the crew.

CAPTAIN

A captain's main role was to choose targets to attack and command during battle.

SURGEON

Someone with a strong stomach and some medical knowledge had to be on-board to treat any diseases or nasty wounds.

PILOT

A good navigator was vital to avoid a ship smashing into rocks or getting lost.

COOK

Disabled pirates often got the job of cooking, but the cook sometimes got called on to be a surgeon as well.

QUARTERMASTER

The quartermaster was the second-in-command. He made sure that orders were obeyed, divided up plunder and flogged crew members for bad behaviour.

MUSICIAN

Musicians played merry tunes while the crew worked, ate and prepared for battle.

CARPENTER

The carpenter had to fix any damage to the ship, making use of whatever he could, because pirates could not visit official ports to get repairs done or stock up on wood.

BOATSWAIN

The boatswain (called the 'bosun') kept the ship in order. He operated the anchor, set the sails and kept the decks clean.

COOPER

The cooper looked after the ship's barrels. Barrels were the best thing to store stuff in at sea. They kept creepy-crawlies out of food and saved water from being wasted.

MASTER GUNNER

The Master Gunner was in charge of all of the cannons, the gunpowder and the shot. Operating a cannon or 'gun' was dangerous work.

Home, Horrible Home

Ships at this time were cramped, smelly and damp, and pirate vessels were no different.

Pirate crews needed enough people to sail the ship. The captain and senior crew members would have their own cabins at the stern (back) of the ship, but the rest would have to sleep wherever they could find space.

There was always the danger of explosions, especially if a shot hit gunpowder stores during a battle or a fire took hold on-board.

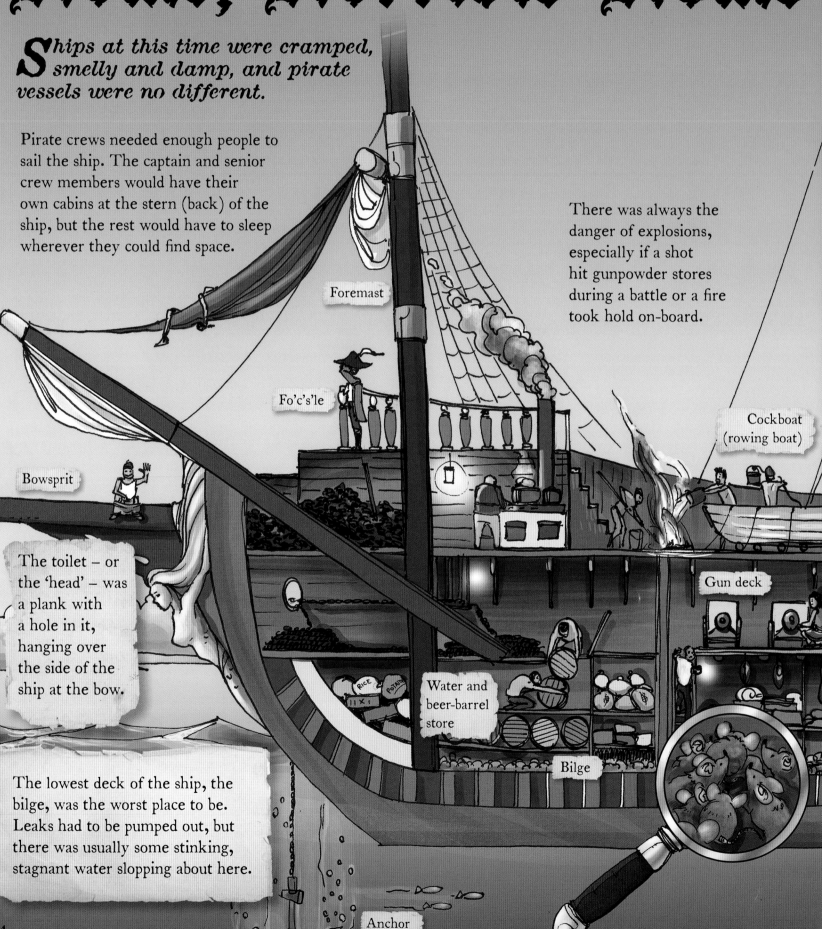

Foremast

Fo'c's'le

Cockboat (rowing boat)

Bowsprit

The toilet – or the 'head' – was a plank with a hole in it, hanging over the side of the ship at the bow.

Gun deck

Water and beer-barrel store

Bilge

The lowest deck of the ship, the bilge, was the worst place to be. Leaks had to be pumped out, but there was usually some stinking, stagnant water slopping about here.

Anchor

Sailors had to climb high in the rigging even in stormy weather, risking a fatal fall. Someone had to stay on watch day and night. If the lookout fell asleep, the ship could smash into rocks or founder on sandbanks.

Mizzenmast

Rigging

Helmsman steering

Poop deck

Mainmast

Quarterdeck

Captain's cabin

Capstan

Main deck

Rudder

Food stores

Keel

Ships crawled with rats and cockroaches. Rats were a dangerous menace, eating the food stores and gnawing through important equipment such as rope. They carried diseases, too.

Get to Work!

Pirates didn't just loll around drinking and playing cards. They had to work hard to keep their ships in order. If not they risked being caught or shipwrecked.

A HAPPY HULL

If the layer of algae and barnacles encrusting the ship's hull got too thick, it could slow the ship down. It was important that the hull was regularly cleaned, which was called 'careening'.

A DANGEROUS JOB

To careen a ship it had to be taken out of the water. The pirates had to find a hidden beach for their DIY session and hope they didn't get caught by an enemy while unable to escape. Here are some of the stinking steps in the smelly hot work of careening:

CAULKING – beating oakum (old rope) between planks and smearing it with hot tar to make it watertight.

GRAVING – painting the underwater parts of the ship with a stinking, boiled-up mixture of animal fat, whale, seal or fish oil, resin and sulphur (which smells like rotten eggs). This cut down on pests such as teredo worms.

PARCELLING – laying long strips of canvas on deck between planks and sealing them with caulk and hot tar.

TEREDO TERROR

Teredo worms, a kind of saltwater clam, would fix themselves to wooden hulls. When they moved on, they left their shells behind, encrusting the ship.

UNLUCKY LOWTHER

In 1723 unlucky pirate Captain George Lowther and his crew were spotted and attacked while careening on a remote Venezuelan island. Lowther was never found, dead or alive!

BAD DIY = STORM DISASTER

Why was it so important to plug gaps in the hull and deck? Because crashing storm waves would put pressure on the hull planks, opening up the gaps and causing leaks. If the leaks got really bad, the ship would sink.

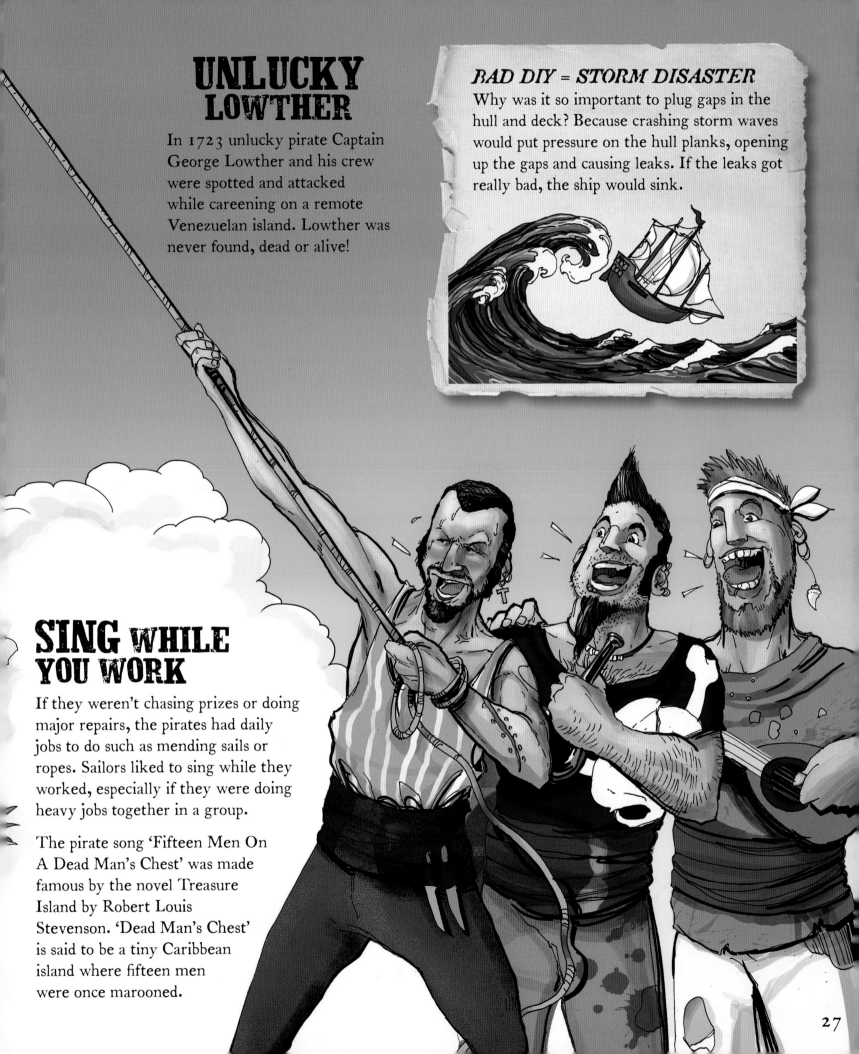

SING WHILE YOU WORK

If they weren't chasing prizes or doing major repairs, the pirates had daily jobs to do such as mending sails or ropes. Sailors liked to sing while they worked, especially if they were doing heavy jobs together in a group.

The pirate song 'Fifteen Men On A Dead Man's Chest' was made famous by the novel Treasure Island by Robert Louis Stevenson. 'Dead Man's Chest' is said to be a tiny Caribbean island where fifteen men were once marooned.

Pirate Town

Pirates needed safe ports where they could anchor to stock up with supplies, sell stolen goods and pick up information to plan their next attack. Most important of all, they needed somewhere to party, pirate-style.

WORLD'S WICKEDEST TOWN

Tortuga Island, off the coast of modern Haiti, was a popular early hiding place for buccaneers. It was a den of villains looking for ways to make money, but the pirates had to flee when the Spanish and French came after them. Many went to Port Royal in Jamaica, which soon got the nickname 'the wickedest city in the world'.

ROUGH AND ROWDY

In pirate times Port Royal was a boom-town filled with gambling dens and taverns. There were so many taverns, there was said to be one for every ten locals! The town was the perfect place to buy or sell stolen goods and slaves.

END OF THE PIER SHOW

Pirates didn't get things all their own way in Port Royal. Some of them were tried and hanged at scarily-named Gallows Point on the edge of town. Infamous pirate villains Charles Vane and Jack Rackham both met their ends here.

PORT ROYAL'S TOP PIRATE

Sir Henry Morgan was Port Royal's most successful pirate. He used it as a base for attacking Spanish towns, got very rich and ran Port Royal just the way he wanted. When he died in 1688 there was a huge funeral procession through Port Royal and ships in the bay fired their guns in his honour.

THE PARTY'S OVER

In 1692 a huge earthquake destroyed the town. The ground was mostly sand, and instantly liquefied, sucking buildings and people down in a terrifying few minutes. Then a tsunami engulfed most of what remained, leaving up to 5,000 people dead.

Diving archaeologists have since found underwater remains of the old town, including lots of drinking tankards and pieces of eight.

Out to Get You!

When European governments decided to stamp out piracy, they hired pirate-hunters to catch crews. These seafarers were often just as bloodthirsty as the men they were sent to capture!

I BEG YOUR PARDON!

During the 1710s and 1720s, the British government decided to crack down on the Caribbean pirates. They offered pardons and set pirate-hunters on those who refused to change their ways.

TOUGH GUY COMES TO TOWN

In 1718 the English sent a tough former privateer called Woodes Rogers to be Governor of Nassau and get rid of the pirates. Pirate Charles Vane gave him a cheeky welcome by firing on his ship as he entered Nassau Harbour! Rogers offered a pardon to anyone who would sign a contract swearing to give up piracy.

BLACKBEARD'S LAST BATTLE

In 1718, pirate Blackbeard supposedly retired, accepted a pardon and settled down in what is now North Carolina, USA. Secretly he was still a pirate, working with a crooked local governor who got a share of Blackbeard's loot in return for protecting him.

On November 22, 1718, two Royal Navy warships under the command of Captain Robert Maynard cornered Blackbeard in Okracoke Inlet. During a fierce battle, Blackbeard was killed. His head was cut off and hung on the bowsprit of Maynard's ship.

THE END OF BLACK BART

In 1722, a warship, the *Swallow*, was sent to hunt down pirate 'Black' Bart Roberts. When Roberts saw the *Swallow*, he mistook it for a prize and sent one of his own ships, the *Ranger*, to attack it.

The *Swallow* captured the *Ranger*, chained up its pirate crew and then went back for a battle with Roberts. Roberts was killed by cannon fire. His men threw his body overboard before surrendering.

WOODES ROGERS – SAVED BY A BOOK

Before Woodes Rogers was a pirate hunter he bought and sold slaves. Towards the end of his life he lost all his money and was thrown in jail. Then the very popular book, *A General History Of The Pyrates*, was published, celebrating his pirate-hunting exploits. He was allowed out of jail and given his old job back as Governor of Nassau.

Pirate Style

Did real-life pirates really dress the way they do in the movies? Check out these pirate style notes!

CLOTHES CRIMES

Pirates stole style ideas. Literally! The scoundrels snatched clothing from prisoners they captured.

CAPTAIN of STYLE

Captain 'Black' Bart Roberts was a famously snappy dresser. He was known for his feathered hats and gold jewellery.

REBEL THREADS

English and French clothing laws stated that only wealthy important people were allowed to wear fine fabrics. Pirate captains delighted in wearing grand clothing to show that they didn't care about these snobby rules.

Wig

Fancy buttons

Crimson velvet coat and breeches

Satin sash across the front of his shirt and round his waist

SAVE IT FOR BEST

Pirates tended to wear their best outfits on shore. At sea they had dangerous and dirty jobs to do, so they preferred practical outfits. A bandana kept sweat out of your eyes and a stolen hat kept the sun off.

Ornate shoe buckles

Stockings

I CAN SEW, YOU KNOW!

Sailors were often good at sewing, and could mend or remake clothes. Some even embroidered as a hobby.

SAILOR SUITS

Seamen who jumped ship from the British Navy usually carried on wearing their Navy clothes for a while. As time went on, the kit would wear out and the pirates would start to look scruffy and smell bad.

Yum...Worms Again!

Food on-board a pirate ship sounds awful. Then again, in those days, there were no fridges to keep food fresh. Even on land many people had terrible diets and often went hungry.

STALE AND SALTY

Fresh food was very hard to preserve and soon started to rot and crawl with maggots. Hunks of meat and fish were packed in barrels of salt to try to stop them going off, making them tough and chewy.

- Some ships kept live chickens, pigs and cows on-board for fresh food. When supplies got low, they would kill the animals and eat them.

- Water didn't stay fresh for long out at sea, so it was mixed with rum, beer or spices to try to make it taste better.

- If pirate crews were really low on food, they would catch and cook the rats that lived below decks.

A FAMILY PICNIC...

Legend has it that female pirate Charlotte de Berry's crew were so hungry when they got marooned on an island, they drew straws to decide who they would eat. The first chosen victim was her husband. Nobody knows if this grisly story is true, but it's certainly one way to eat a 'family meal'!

A PIRATE MENU

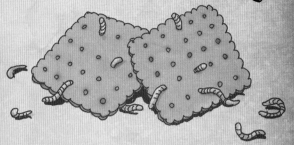

HARD TACK

Dry square biscuits made from flour, water and salt. When they were stored they got infested with weevils (a type of beetle), earning the nickname 'worm castles'.

SALMAGUNDY

A pirate's treat! Salted fish and boiled onions served with anything else that was available, such as turtle meat, pork or chicken, bird's eggs, oil, wine and shellfish.

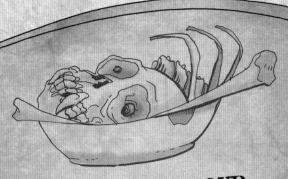

PIRATE BONE SOUP

A broth made from boiled-up animal bones.

TURTLE MEAT AND EGGS

Pirates loved to eat turtles because they were easy to catch and the flesh was soft. There was just one grim side effect – the delicacy made their poo black and their pee green!

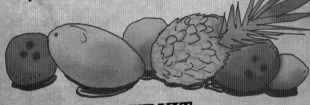

FRUIT

If they anchored near land, pirates would go on shore to look for fresh fruit. Without fruit and veg they risked dying from the dreaded scurvy.

DESPERATE DINING

In 1670, Sir Henry Morgan's crew were stranded on the shore. They had to eat tree bark, leaves and even their leather satchels.

The sailors cut the leather into strips, soaked it to soften it, then cooked it over a fire. It must still have tasted horrible!

Party Pirates

Pirates tended to be a rowdy lot. Their idea of a good time was to have a riotous knees-up with their shipmates.

GOING EXTREME ON SHORE

When pirates docked, they chose hideout towns such as Port Royal or Tortuga. These safe harbours were the perfect place to gamble, smoke and party, in return for cash. By the end of a visit, the crew were likely to go back to sea with their pockets empty.

Pirates smoked ashore because they generally only chewed tobacco on deck, in case they set fire to their ship.

'THREE SHEETS TO THE WIND'

This sailing-related phrase means unsteady because of drink, like a ship floundering when important ropes (sheets) aren't properly holding the sails in place.

IN THE PIRATE'S INN

Here are some favourite pirate tipples.

RUMFUSTIAN

Sugar, beer, gin, sherry and raw eggs, all mixed together and served hot.

BUMBOO

Water, nutmeg, sugar and rum.

KILL-DEVIL

An extra-strong rum punch served in the pirate port of Port Royal.

GROG

Watered-down rum. The English word 'groggy', meaning ill or dizzy, comes from 'grog'.

EXPLOSIVE TIME

In 1669, Sir Henry Morgan gathered his fleet of ships together and held a captains' meeting on-board his ship, the *Oxford*. The crews partied and somehow a stray spark ignited a barrel of gunpowder, which blew up.

BEST PIRATE PARTY EVER

In 1718, pirate Captains Charles Vane and Blackbeard met up at Ocracoke, in present-day North Carolina, USA. The crews held a wild party on the beach, which went on for several days. Locals say that Blackbeard still haunts his party beach.

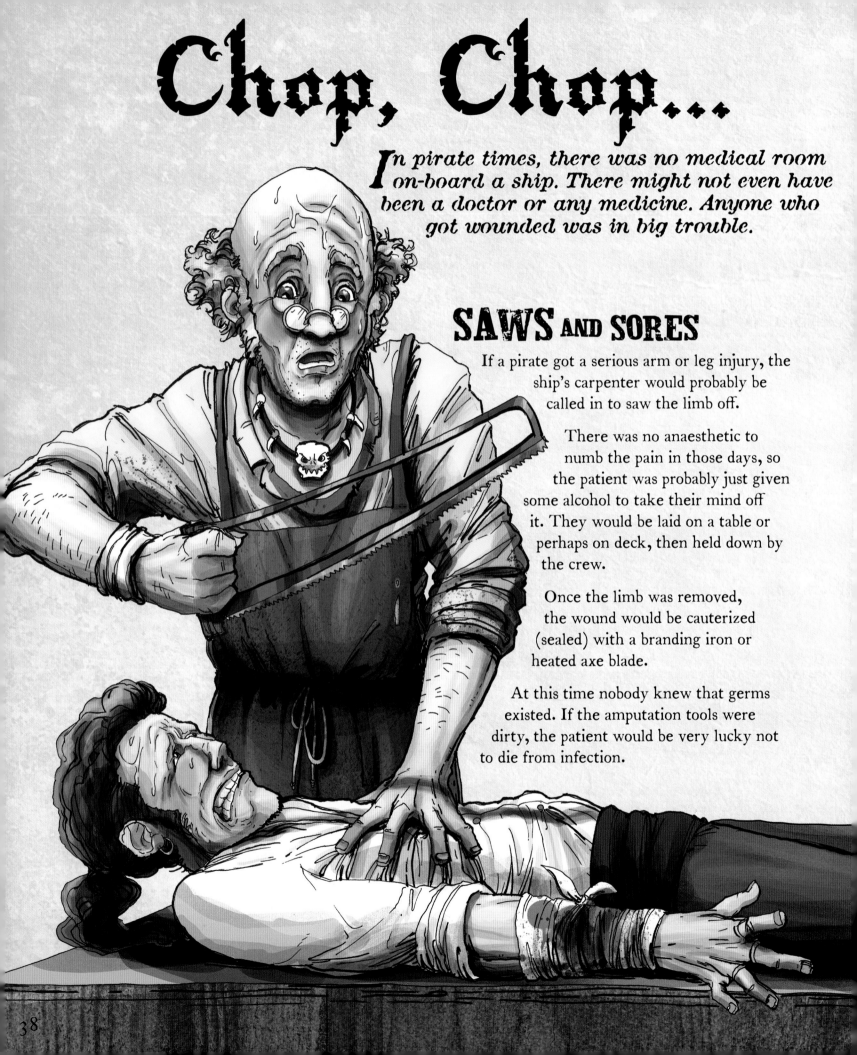

Chop, Chop...

In pirate times, there was no medical room on-board a ship. There might not even have been a doctor or any medicine. Anyone who got wounded was in big trouble.

SAWS AND SORES

If a pirate got a serious arm or leg injury, the ship's carpenter would probably be called in to saw the limb off.

There was no anaesthetic to numb the pain in those days, so the patient was probably just given some alcohol to take their mind off it. They would be laid on a table or perhaps on deck, then held down by the crew.

Once the limb was removed, the wound would be cauterized (sealed) with a branding iron or heated axe blade.

At this time nobody knew that germs existed. If the amputation tools were dirty, the patient would be very lucky not to die from infection.

LEG OVERBOARD!

Having an arm or leg removed was a very dangerous operation. If a pirate survived that awful ordeal, he might get a hook or a wooden leg, crudely made from a spare ship's plank. Or he would have to struggle with a crutch.

The first peg-leg pirate was Francois Le Clerc, a French privateer. Despite losing a leg in 1549, he carried on raiding the Spanish until he died in 1563.

FIRST CATCH YOUR DOCTOR

If a ship's surgeon was captured from another ship, he would be kept as a hostage to help the pirates. Privateers had an official government licence so it was easier for them to employ an official doctor.

TREASURE CHEST INDEED

A ship's medicine chest was a valuable prize. It contained ointments, medicines, dressings and bandages. Chests sometimes contained instructions written by a trained doctor, but many sailors could not read. They'd have to guess and hope for the best!

Blackbeard once stole a ship sailing out of Charleston, in present-day South Carolina, with wealthy families on-board. He threatened to hang them all unless the townspeople sent him a medicine chest. Once he got his precious booty, he released the terrified prisoners (though not before stealing their clothes and jewels).

Sick as a Pirate

Pirates were a tough bunch, which was a good job when you look at some of the awful illnesses they had to put up with.

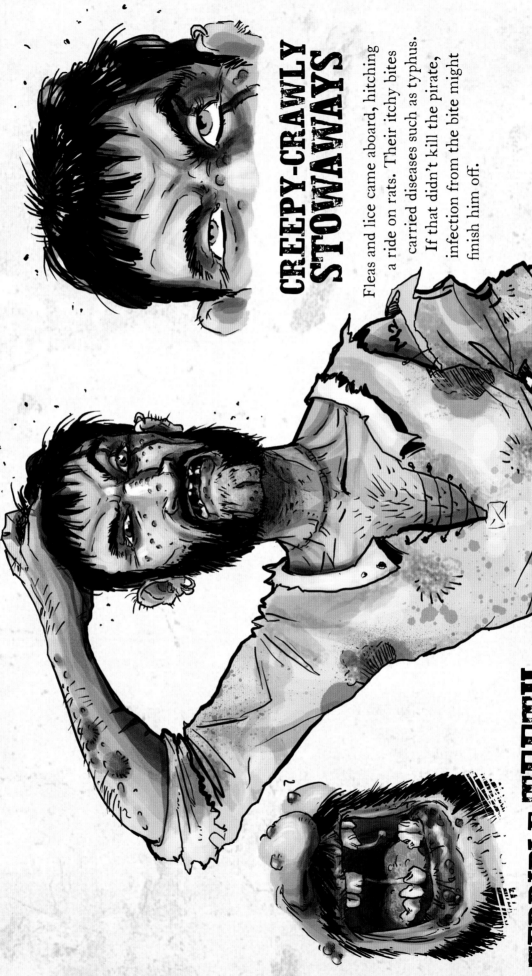

CREEPY-CRAWLY STOWAWAYS

Fleas and lice came aboard, hitching a ride on rats. Their itchy bites carried diseases such as typhus. If that didn't kill the pirate, infection from the bite might finish him off.

TERRIBLE TEETH

Pirates never brushed their teeth and there were no dentists. When a tooth rotted, it had to be pulled out with pliers.

PHWOOR ME HEARTIES!

How did pirates smell? Dreadful! Sweating in tropical heat and wearing the same clothes with no chance of a bath must have made them a stinky bunch.

SCURVY SEADOGS

On long voyages it was hard to get fruit and vegetables to eat. This led to a lack of vitamin C, which caused the dreaded scurvy. Scurvy-sufferers got bleeding gums and blackened, sore-covered skin. Their limbs seized up and they often went mad, too.

PEG LEG PAY

Pirates were paid compensation by their crew if they lost a limb, an eye or a finger. The highest payout was for a lost right arm or leg.

DEADLY DRINK

Beastly bacteria lurked in stale drinking water, causing dysentery and cholera, which could both lead to a deadly case of the runs. If their water ran out, pirates would sometimes drink their wee instead!

HARD TIMES

Pirates weren't the only ones that struggled to stay healthy. In the Golden Age there were no antibiotics or vaccines. Anyone would be lucky to reach old age.

We're Behind You!

Pirates had some sneaky ways of targeting prizes and creeping up on their victims...

I SPY

Pirates tried to get information about when and where valuable ships were sailing. They hung around taverns and coffeehouses in ports, hoping to hear interesting news. Sometimes they questioned the prisoners they captured to discover secret plans.

SEA SNEAKING

Pirates sailed just outside of the main shipping routes, hoping to find lone merchant ships leaving or entering port, loaded with goodies. They preferred to sail along coastlines so they could hide in coves and set up ambushes.

FAST AND SMART

Pirates liked to use coastal schooners – fast, light boats that were very manoeuvrable. Sometimes they would creep up on ships in even smaller craft. In 1635, it is believed that French buccaneer Pierre le Grand and a crew of twenty-eight captured an anchored Spanish flagship by rowing up to it and silently climbing aboard.

SHIP SHADOWING

Once they spotted a possible target ship, the pirates would shadow it, trying to work out if it was worth attacking or not. They studied the hull of their potential target to see if it was riding high in the water or low, in which case it would probably be full of cargo to steal.

SURPRISE!

Once they got close enough to their enemy, the pirates would hoist their flag, a signal to surrender or die. The crew would scream and wave their weapons to frighten the victim's vessel into surrendering without a fight.

Fearsome Flags

Pirates liked to sneak up on victims and terrify them into surrendering without the risk of a battle. A pirate flag was a scary signal. It meant 'Surrender quickly or die!'.

RED TO BLACK

The first pirate flags had a red background symbolizing bloodshed – meaning that anyone who fought back would be executed. The flag had a French buccaneer name – the *Jolie Rouge* – a nasty joke meaning 'pretty red'. Red flags were soon replaced with black, symbolizing death.

PRETTY HORRIBLE

The pirate flag eventually got the nickname 'Jolly Roger'. This was probably the English version of the French name, but might also come from the English slang 'Old Roger', meaning the Devil.

SURPRISE!

Sometimes a pirate ship would fly a false flag called a *ruse de guerre*, pretending to be friendly. When it got close enough to attack, the crew would hoist the pirate flag to force a scared surrender.

SURRENDER WHEN YOU SEE THIS SIGN

Each pirate captain had his own fearsome flag.

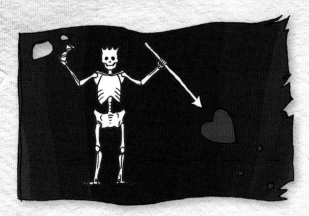

The message of Blackbeard's flag was 'You don't have much time. Surrender or die!'

Stede Bonnet's flag was covered with scary symbols.

Bart Roberts had several flags, including this one, symbolizing 'Your time is running out'.

This flag showed Roberts' hatred of the ports of Martinique and Barbados.

The famous flag of Calico Jack Rackham.

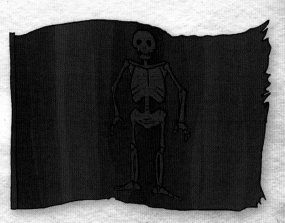

This bloodthirsty flag was for a bloodthirsty pirate, Edward Low.

Attack!

Once a pirate ship drew alongside a target, the decks quickly got smoky, slippery and smelly. The battle was on!

1 Grappling irons – metal hooks on the end of ropes – were thrown into the rigging to pull the ship close.

2 Most sailors went barefoot, so the pirates threw spiked metal pieces called caltrops on-deck to pierce their feet.

3 The attackers lobbed hand grenades made by filling empty wine bottles or coconut shells with gunpowder and bits of metal.

4 Sometimes they burnt yellow sulphur to make a smokescreen. It smelt like stinky, rotten eggs.

5 Pirates attacked masts to stop their victims from getting away. They had to be careful however – a damaged vessel was no use to them!

6 Sailors tried to stop the pirates boarding by greasing the decks or scattering dried peas.

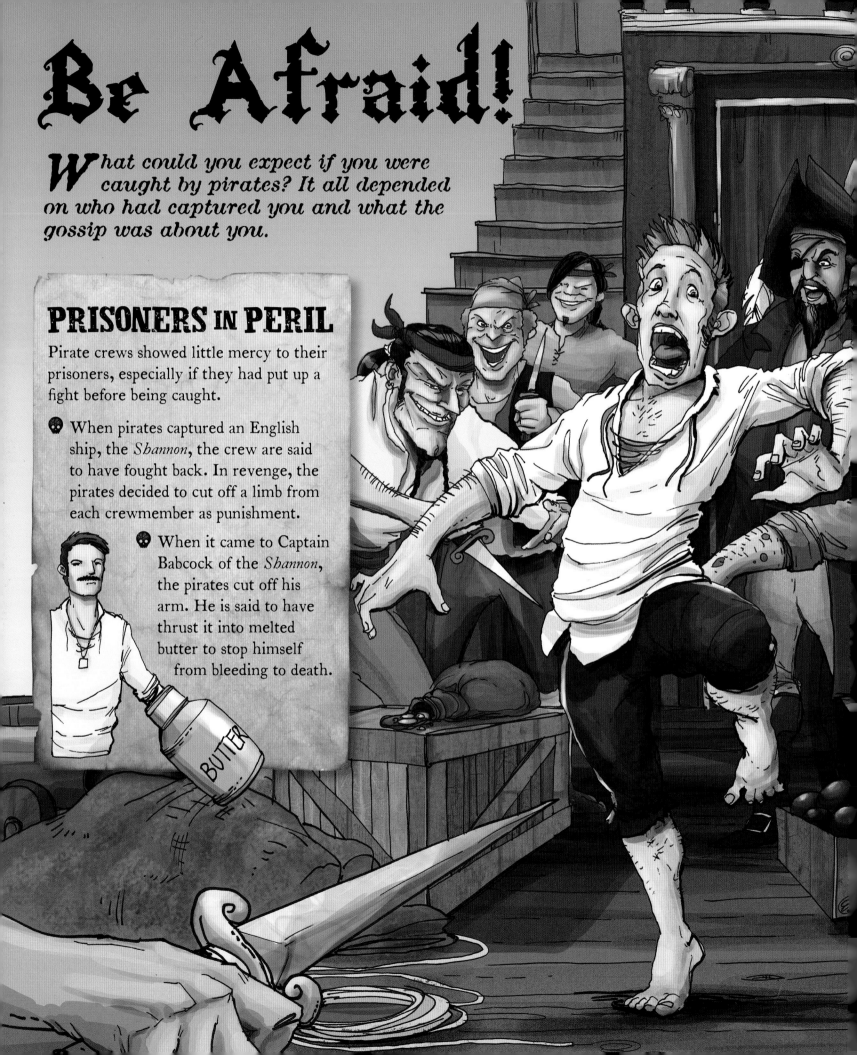

Be Afraid!

What could you expect if you were caught by pirates? It all depended on who had captured you and what the gossip was about you.

PRISONERS IN PERIL

Pirate crews showed little mercy to their prisoners, especially if they had put up a fight before being caught.

☠ When pirates captured an English ship, the *Shannon*, the crew are said to have fought back. In revenge, the pirates decided to cut off a limb from each crewmember as punishment.

☠ When it came to Captain Babcock of the *Shannon*, the pirates cut off his arm. He is said to have thrust it into melted butter to stop himself from bleeding to death.

BUTTER

CAPTAINS
GET CAUGHT

Once a ship was captured, the pirates would ask the crew what their captain was like. If the sailors said he was cruel, he was doomed to a nasty end.

Some captured captains were made to 'sweat', which meant running round and round between decks while pirate musicians played a jig. The rest of the crew jabbed the victim in the backside with knives and swords to make him go faster, until he collapsed.

PIRATE'S REVENGE

Pirates vowed to torture and kill anyone who betrayed them, and they punished towns that held out against piracy. Some say Bart Roberts hanged the Governor of Martinique after he supported pirate-hunters.

DID PIRATES MAKE PRISONERS WALK THE PLANK?

Yes, but rarely and not during the Golden Age. Pirates were more likely to throw people overboard. In 1822, captured Captain William Smith was apparently made to walk a plank.

Lots of Loot

Once pirates caught a ship, they stripped it of its goods to share amongst themselves. Sometimes however, they couldn't resist cheating each other. After all, they were rotten thieves!

When a vessel was captured, the booty was shared out among the crew. Everyone was supposed to get equal shares, except for the most important people, who were given extra.

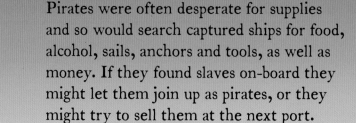

Pirates were often desperate for supplies and so would search captured ships for food, alcohol, sails, anchors and tools, as well as money. If they found slaves on-board they might let them join up as pirates, or they might try to sell them at the next port.

SHIPWRECK SECRETS

The wreck of the pirate ship, the *Whydah*, was found in 1984 off the coast of New England, USA, where it sank in 1717. Among the objects recovered by divers was gold jewellery that had been hacked apart with a knife to divide it equally.

SIGN AND SHARE

Apparently some crewmembers cheated pirate 'Black' Bart Roberts out of his loot, sailing off with it in the night. That's why he wrote down some rules, and made all his crewmen sign it.

BIG BOOTY

According to one tale, Captain Henry Every captured the biggest pirate treasure hoard ever recorded. After a fierce battle in the Indian Ocean, Every and a fleet of pirates captured the treasure ship of the Grand Moghul of India. The greatest prize on-board was a gold saddle encrusted with gemstones.

X Marks the Spot

Thanks to books and films, we think of pirates burying their booty and drawing secret treasure maps. Did anyone really do this, and if so where should we start digging?

BURIED FOR A BIT

Sir Francis Drake once robbed gold and silver from a train of wagons travelling through the mainland of Panama. When he got back to the coast he discovered that his ships had been chased off by the Spanish and he was stuck on shore. Drake buried the loot and set sail on a makeshift raft to find them. A few hours later, he was able to return and dig up the riches.

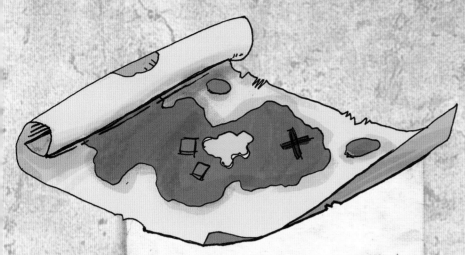

GONE TO THE GRAVE

English privateer Thomas Jones retired a wealthy man and went to live in present day Long Island, New York. After his death it was rumoured that he had buried his treasure on his land. Nobody ever found it. Supposedly, one frustrated treasure seeker scratched a poem on Jones's headstone:

Beneath this stone repose the bones of Pirate Jones. This briny well contains the shell. The rest's in Hell!

CAPTAIN KIDD'S SECRET

When Captain Kidd was hanged he took his secrets with him. Before he was arrested he was said to have buried mounds of gold and coins somewhere near Gardiner's Island, New York. Some of it was recovered at the time, but people have been hunting for Kidd's secret hoard ever since!

WHERE DID IT GO?

After Blackbeard's death, a search of his ships and of his pirate base at Ocracoke, turned up sugar, wine, cocoa, a barrel of ink and a bale of cotton. Where was the rest of his treasure? Perhaps he had spent it all!

Marooned!

Any pirate who upset his colleagues was likely to find himself left somewhere far away from help, with the choice of waiting to die or killing himself.

HIGH AND DRY

Marooning meant stranding someone on a deserted isle, with just a little food and drink, possibly enough to last only one day. Some stretches of sand were even covered with water at high tide, leaving the pirate to drown or get eaten by sharks.

The victim was usually left with a pistol to shoot himself rather than face a slow death.

Sometimes captured prisoners were marooned. In 1821 near Cuba, Captain Barnabas Lincoln and some of his crew were abandoned on an island by pirates. Luckily, some of them escaped on a raft and brought back help.

LEAVE ME HERE

Alexander Selkirk was a privateer who chose to be marooned, when he thought the ship he was on was unsafe to sail. He survived on the island of Juan Fernandez for many years.

Selkirk was the real-life inspiration for *Robinson Crusoe*.

He's a Her!

A few pirates were wild and wicked women. In 1720, Anne Bonney and Mary Read got thrown into a Jamaican jail for their bloodthirsty ways. Here's their shocking story.

I LIKE PIRATES

Anne Bonney was a wild teenager who ran away from what is now Charlestown, USA, to marry a pirate called James Bonney. Legend has it she later ran off with another pirate, Calico Jack Rackham.

GO, GIRLS!

Anne went on Jack's ship disguised as a man, because women were supposed to bring bad luck. It was there that she met Mary Read, another pirate who was secretly a woman.

PROPER CHOPPER

Before she became a pirate, Mary Read joined the English army disguised as a boy, fighting skillfully and getting promoted. She sailed to the Caribbean before winning a duel with another member of Jack's crew.

FIGHT LIKE A MAN

The story goes that Jack and his crew were drunk below deck when their ship was attacked by pirate hunters. The pirates proved useless with their swords, leaving the women to lead the fighting. However, they were all overpowered. Jack and his crewmen were all caught and hanged, and the women were condemned to die, too.

BUT THEN...

Mary died of a fever in a damp, stinking jail before she could be hanged, but Anne's fate is a mystery. She may have been given a pardon and gone home to have Jack's child.

GIRL-FREE ZONE

'Black' Bart Roberts was no fan of females. He banned his crew on pain of death from inviting their lady friends to sea.

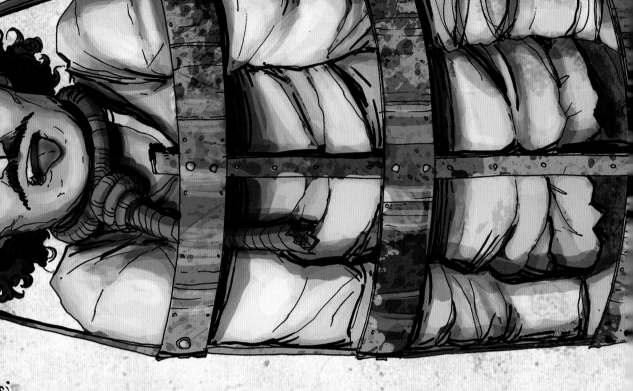

Caught!

*T*he Golden Age had begun with European nations using pirates to help them attack their enemies, but by 1713 those same countries wanted to stamp out piracy because it was harming their trade.

WASHED AWAY

Up until 1700 English pirates were transported back to London if they were caught. They stood trial and were hanged at Execution Dock, Wapping, on the north bank of the Thames. They were hung at low tide and afterwards their bodies were left for the tide to rise and wash over them three times. Then they were cut down and buried in an unmarked grave.

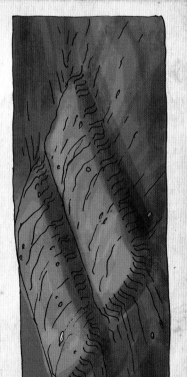

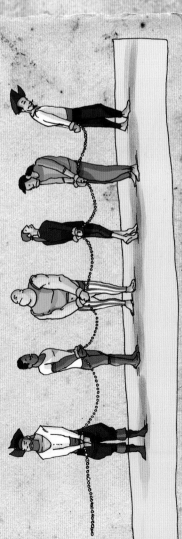

FEARSOME FACTS

- Some executed pirates were dissected by doctors for medical research.
- The Spanish authorities executed pirates. The French often sent them into slavery.
- Between 1716 and 1726, over 400 pirates were hanged.

FOR ALL TO SEE

After pirate Captain William Kidd was tried and hanged in London, his body was hung in a gibbet, a custom-made iron cage, at Tilbury Point on the banks of the Thames. He was left there for three years for everyone to see as they sailed in and out of London as a warning to any would-be pirates.

DEAD SMART

Pirates liked to dress in their best finery when they were sent to the gallows to be hung. Sometimes they wound ribbons round their clothing to create a showy effect as they swung.

HANGING TOGETHER

In 1700 British law changed, so that pirates could be tried and executed wherever they were caught. Sometimes whole crews were hanged at the same time. In 1722 the British Admiralty tried 169 of Bart Roberts' crew, then executed fifty-two of them on the Guinea Coast.

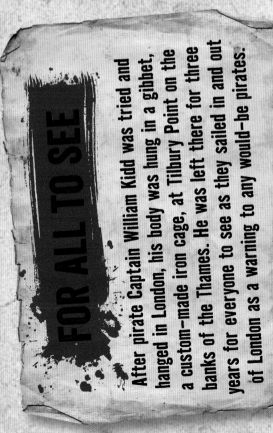

Pirates Go East

Tough pirates infested the China seas from the 1600s to the 1800s. They did things differently to the Caribbean crews, but were just as ruthless and greedy!

FIGHTING FLEETS

The Chinese pirates sailed in large, well-organised fleets. They sailed ships called 'junks', with sails made of bamboo matting. These pirates were so powerful they controlled big areas of China's coastline, ruling through violence and threats.

By the mid-1800s, Chinese piracy came to an end when the British Navy used steam-powered warships to smash their fleets.

SHE WHO MUST BE OBEYED

One of China's most powerful pirate chiefs, a woman called Ching Shih, commanded hundreds of junks. She was so powerful, no one dared to break her rules.

China

Japan

HEADHUNTERS

The Asian islands of Borneo and Sumatra were the haunts of seagoing pirates who liked to shrink down their enemy's heads and display them as trophies at home.

Sumatra

Borneo

Australia

AMPUTATION – cutting off of a wounded limb, such as an arm or leg.

ARTICLES OF AGREEMENT – a code that pirates had to sign. It was a list of dos and don'ts on-board.

BILGE – the very bottom deck of a ship. A damp and smelly place.

BOATSWAIN – the crewmember in charge of keeping the ship in good shape. Pronounced 'bosun'.

BOWSPRIT – the spar of wood sticking out from the bow (front) of a ship.

BUCCANEERS – pirates in the late 1500s who originated on the Caribbean island of Hispaniola.

BUMBOO – a mixture of water, nutmeg, sugar and rum.

CALTROPS – spiky metal pieces thrown onto the deck during an attack, designed to injure people who stepped on them.

CAREENING – hauling a ship onto a beach at high tide, to scrape barnacles from the hull and repair it.

CAULKING – beating oakum (old rope) between planks and smearing it with hot tar to make a ship watertight.

CAUTERIZING – sealing a wound up to stop it bleeding.

COOPER – the crewmember who made and repaired barrels.

DOUBLOON – a gold coin manufactured by the Spanish in South America.

FLAGSHIP – the most important ship in an armada, carrying the fleet's commander.

FLOGGING – the punishment of a severe whipping.

GALLEON – a big, heavy cargo ship.

GALLOWS – a wooden frame with a noose, used for hanging criminals.

GIBBET – an iron cage made for an executed pirate, to hang his body up in a public place as a warning to others.

GOLDEN AGE – the era of pirate activity from 1690 to 1730.

GRAPPLING IRONS – metal hooks on the end of ropes, thrown into the rigging to pull a ship close during an attack.

GRAVING – painting the underwater parts of the ship with a boiled-up mixture of animal fat, resin and sulphur, to protect it.

GROG – watered-down rum.

HARD TACK – dry square ship's biscuits made from flour, water and salt.

HEAD – the ship's toilet, a plank with a hole in it hung over the side.

JOLIE ROUGE – pirate flag with a red background, used by early buccaneers.

JOLLY ROGER – the slang name for a pirate flag.

JUNK – a Chinese ship with sails made of bamboo matting.

KEEL-HAULING – the punishment of being tied to a rope and pulled under the ship's hull from one side to the other.

LETTERS OF MARQUE – official government papers giving permission for privately-owned ships to attack enemy countries.

MAROONING – being left on a deserted island as a punishment, with just a little food and water, possibly enough to last only one day.

MASTER GUNNER – the pirate in charge of all of the guns, gunpowder and the shot.

MUTINY – a crew disobeying a captain, perhaps killing him or setting him adrift in a boat.

PARCELLING – laying long strips of canvas on deck between planks and sealing them with caulk (old rope) and hot tar.

PIECES OF EIGHT – silver coins manufactured by the Spanish in South America.

PILOT – a ship's navigator.

PIRATE BONE SOUP – a broth made from boiled-up animal bones.

PRESS-GANGED – to be kidnapped and forced to join the British Navy.

PRIVATEER – a sailor with a privately-owned ship, licensed by a government to attack the ships and settlements of enemy countries.

PRIZE – a captured ship.

QUARTERMASTER – the second-in-command on a pirate ship. He made sure orders were obeyed, divided up plunder and punished crewmembers for bad behaviour.

RUSE DE GUERRE – a fake ship's flag.

SALMAGUNDY – a plateful of available food such as salted fish, eggs, turtle meat, pork or chicken, bird's eggs, oil, wine and shellfish.

SCHOONER – a fast, light boat that was very manoeuvrable.

SCURVY – a fatal disease suffered by sailors who didn't eat any vitamin C (found in vegetables and fruit).

SPANISH MAIN – the coast of northern South America, controlled by the Spanish.

STERN – the back of a ship.

TEREDO WORMS – a kind of mollusc (snail) found in tropical waters, prone to fixing themselves to wooden hulls.

Index